I AM POWER: Divine, Powerful Affirmations that Can Change Your Life One Moment at a Time. Copyright © 2019, Daya Devi-Doolin, Padaran Publications, Deltona, FL 32725.

All Rights Reserved, including the right to reproduce the book, or any portion thereof, in any form such as by any means, graphic, electronic, or mechanical, electronic or mechanical, including photocopying, recording, taping or by any information storage or retrieval system without prior permission of the Publisher, except for the inclusion of brief quotations in a review. The First Edition of A Course in Miracles is now free from copyright and we have permission to use.

Publisher's Note

The Publisher and Author shall have neither liability nor responsibility to any person or organization with respect to any loss or damage caused or alleged to be caused directly or indirectly by the information contained in this book. The purpose of this book is to educate, entertain and stimulate. This book is sold with the understanding that the Publisher and Author are not involved in offering legal, medical or psychological service.

ISBN: 978 1 877945 23 6
Library of Congress Card Catalog Number   2019941793
First Edition   1 2 3 4 5 6 7 8 9 10
Editor – Jacqueline Seal
Sales: www.padaran.com   Email: padaran@padaran.com
Telephone: (386) 479-8151
Graphic Designer: Daria Brennan www.beegraphica.com

Printed in the United States of America
Padaran Publications
1794 N. Acadian Dr. Deltona, FL 32725

I AM POWER

Divine, Powerful Affirmations
That Can Change Your Life
One Moment at a Time

Daya Devi-Doolin

Padaran Publications
Deltona, FL 32725

Books Written by Daya Devi-Doolin

I AM Power: *Divine, Powerful Affirmations that Can Change Your Life One Moment at a Time.*
Grow Thin While You Sleep!
Yoga, Meditation and Spirituality for African American Community: If You Can Breathe, You Can Do Yoga!
The Only Way Out Is In: The Secrets of the 14 Realms to Love, Happiness and Success!
Super Vita-Minds: How to Stop Saying I Hate You...To Yourself
Americans Saving Ourselves Together: How to Thrive in the 21st Century
Dabney's Handbook on A Course in Miracles
All I Need to Know....Is Inside (A Pocket Bite Book with cartoons)
Dabney, Dormck & Wiggles' Slakaduman Adventures
Dormck and the Temple of the Healing Light
Sikado's Star of Aragon (Dabney & Dormck Adventures)

Books Written by Chris & Daya Devi-Doolin

Hidden Manna: How You Too Can Interpret Your Dreams
Returning to the Source
Smile America
Attention Healing Centers, Schools of Spiritual Growth, and Organizations: Quantity discounts are available on bulk purchases of Daya Devi-Doolin's book for educational purposes or fund raising. For information, please contact: www.padaran.com or call (386) 479-8151. We thank you for your support and bless you in your growth.

Table of Contents

Foreword by Felicia Benzo		i
Preface by Damiana Rosery		ii
Introduction		iii
Chapter 1	What is Fear?	1
Chapter 2	What is Ego?	7
Chapter 3	What Does Sickness Offer You?	9
Chapter 4	Practicing the Holy Instant	12
Chapter 5	How to Give Yourself a Spiritual Facelift!	15
Chapter 6	How to Overcome Depression	17
Chapter 7	How to Get What I Want and Not What I Don't Want!	20
Chapter 8	Did I Really Ask for This?	23
Chapter 9	Creating My Heaven on Earth	26
Chapter 10	How to Manifest Total Healing	29
Chapter 11	How to Empower Myself	35
Chapter 12	How to Live the Life I Want	39
Chapter 13	How Do I Access My I AM Power?	42
Chapter 14	God's Prescription For Me is Perfect Health & Wealth	49
Chapter 15	Our Universal Cellphone	59
Chapter 16	Freeze Negative Energy	66
Chapter 17	True Visualization: Using Your Body as a Dowsing Tool	73
Summary		82
Journal Pages		
Recommended Bibliography		

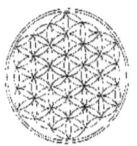

Foreword

Firstly, it is an honor to be asked by Daya Devi-Doolin to write the Foreword for her latest book, I Am Power. She has been a friend, mentor, giver and teacher. Meeting this quiet, gentle, soft spoken soul is an experience in itself, but when you engage with her, great wisdom and POWER become evident.

Her loving kindness is surpassed only by her Divine presence.

I have read all of her books and have learned from and been inspired by them. I highly recommend that you read them. She has outdone herself with I Am Power. It is a peaceful read.

We all have thoughts and feelings which disempower us. However, the challenge is how to release ourselves. I Am Power is a road map for spiritual release. It provides the thinking and the words for us to release our own Divine power and be what we are created to be. Thank you, my friend Daya, for being the teacher and inspiration that you are created to be.

Felicia Benzo, Author -
Raising Kings, Published
by Hustle U Inc.

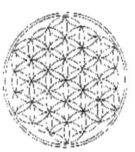

Preface

    This book contains powerful divine affirmations, words of vibrational healing that come from within and a concise blend of affirmations from some of my other metaphysical books.

    These collections of affirmations and quotes are also from the responses of testimonials of those affirmations that directly affected the readers in profound ways which released them from their self-imposed prisons, spiritually, mentally, physically and emotionally.

    I have woven my personal experiences into these chapters to show how I used certain divine principles and Universal Laws to solve my personal situations. I have given the reader techniques and perspectives that they can employ to bring about the divine manifestation they desire to see but don't quite know how – yet.

    Many people don't thoroughly realize that their words create their reality but the fact is, the power of words do. They are becoming aware that there must be a better way even if they don't know what that is. They wonder why their lives don't bring about a peace and a cohesiveness that they see happening to others around them. They read books and books about abundance and prosperity and listen to hundreds of audio books but still don't get it. They don't get that the intention they put behind their words, the force and focus behind their words and thoughts create the undesired or desired end.

    My intention is to help the reader see what they really want to see in their lives and not what they don't want to see.

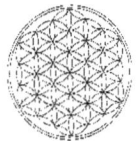

Introduction

October 4, 2018 this book was birthed on the anniversary date of my brother Lee's passing. I sat in meditation on the porch that morning and tuned into him. I asked what message he had for me. Later that day a yoga student of mine, Damiana Rosery, said I ought to think about doing a book of my past quotes that have been very helpful in changing people's minds about their power. I said, you are right. I will start today, though I did not have any plans of writing another book.

The yoga student I mentioned earlier, Damiana, had contacted me with quite a beautiful story. She said she had been given a box of books for free. The book on the top of the pile was entitled "Super Vita-Minds: How to Stop Saying I Hate You…To Yourself", by Daya Devi-Doolin. She picked that one first to read and fell in love with it because the words rang true for her spirit to start expanding to receive her good.

She contacted me somehow and we became friends on Facebook. She told me how all the affirmations written in that book were helping her tremendously to change her thinking about her life. She started writing some of these on index cards for herself to have them close to her. It turned out her parents live in the same city I live in and close by so she could easily stop by and meet with me. Instead it worked out that she signed up to take Gentle Hatha Yoga classes with me at our yoga center location. Here is her story as she relayed it to me.

"What a magical journey! I came to meet Daya in September, 2018, by the divine guidance of our creator, Great Spirit! A friend contacted me, and told me he decided to give up his spiritual path, and informed me he has a box filled with books. I accepted his gift, and little did I know the new adventure ahead of me. The first book I picked up and started reading was titled, "Super Vita Minds – How to Stop Saying I Hate You to Yourself" by Daya Devi-Doolin. This book literally changed my life in so many ways!

I remember reading the title, saying to myself quietly, "I don't hate myself." Well, once I began the program, I realized my love for myself was being met with several conditions, such as, I love myself when I become my ideal weight, or I love myself when my relationship improves with my partner. I discovered, I am worthy of all of these things right now. The negative thought forms towards myself was limiting my ability of creating the life I truly wanted. My higher self knew that it was time for change.

I started Daya's 40 day program by surrendering my will to Great Spirit. I wrote down affirmations on index cards, and incorporated them into my daily practice from the book to include "I am" statements, along with gratitude and forgiveness mantras, and it truly works! After reading Daya's book, I discovered she and her family live only five minutes away from my parents' house. My parents recently moved to Deltona over the summer to be close to us and their grandchildren.

I felt called to connect with Daya and meet with her, and so I did at her next weekly yoga class. Being in Daya's presence, she is an authentic soul, living with the "I Am Presence", and she illuminates so much love and joy in her heart!

Shortly before meeting with Daya I took a break from my path as a healer. I knew there were more layers of healing I needed to work on within myself. My friend was in the hospital battling brain tumors, another friend and shaman mentor crossed over the rainbow bridge, and another friend gave up their spiritual path. I kept getting the message that I am supposed to stand strong on my own, but didn't know how. My Spirit guides moved on, and I felt very alone at the time. I later discovered I am strong enough to face any adversity, and I am. The Holy Spirit was showing me that I can release my fears, and I was reminded I am not just my body, but instead my mind.

I can choose the life I want, and it starts with my thoughts. Change can be uncomfortable for anyone, so generally at first my mind was adjusting to letting go of the ego, and letting the Holy Spirit reprogram and plant new seeds of growth. I had an awakening moment. I opened my eyes for the first time and was filled with tears of joy and gratitude.

Nothing on the outside changed, nor my circumstances, but instead I changed my inner landscape (as I like to call it). I felt true peace from deep within my soul, and I knew everything is going to be okay.

After sharing with Daya of my enlightenment, we discovered my new found awareness was changing me from the inside out!

Several good opportunities starting taking place in my life, and my relationships were improving. Great Spirit spoke to me, and said, "It's about time, I have been waiting for you" with a sense of humor, during a time of my spiritual growth! I told Daya the affirmations in her book were so powerful for me! My profound changes and encouragement inspired her to write her ninth book titled "I AM POWER."

I am so very grateful to be on this journey with you Daya, and I look forward to making this book a part of my daily practice, along with the rest of your spiritual awakening books. Keep on growing consciousness for spiritual growth of all, for the greater good, and so it is. Aho!"
With Love,
Angie Sherman,
www.Elysiumnatural.com

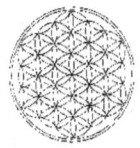

Chapter 1

What Is Fear?

What is fear? Nothing. According to A Course in Miracles, "Nothing unreal exists." What Can Harm You? Nothing. What is there to fear? "There is nothing to Fear." (ACIM). "There are NO Neutral Thoughts.", "All thoughts produce after their own kind." (ACIM).

Thought is Energy. Thoughts are things! Thoughts have form that are invisible but nonetheless have the power to manifest whatever we hold to strongly in our belief. Thoughts have power. They are substance. Thought is the inherited gift we have been given through our One Source.

Our consciousness is The Door, The Way and The Life through which all life springs in our world. My divine suggestion for freeing ourselves of fear is to realize, the thought we have entertained in our consciousness is accepted and then our intention behind that thought moves forward because of our belief or emotion to harbor that thought. It is planted like a seed into our subconscious mind and acted upon through our focus.

The action steps are revealed and followed by us. We then reap the results (manifestation) that were created as we had our initial thought. The Law of Cause and Effect goes into effect the moment we have any one thought. Use this gift of knowing the truth for a Life Without Fear!

Formula Simplified: Thought = Intention = Belief = Action = Result (TIBAR)

You might wonder how can I free myself from fearful thoughts? Holding the following words that are most sacred in your consciousness will free you because there can be no place for fear when you do. Fear will have to take up residence somewhere else because you cannot hold doubt and faith in your mind at the same time. You can know that "The Holy Spirit is my only invited guest" or "Fear is the stranger here" or "In my defenselessness lies my safety." ACIM & Dabney's Handbook On A Course In Miracles, Daya Devi-Doolin. I would also suggest that you might read, "Super Vita-Minds: How to Stop Saying I Hate You…To Yourself" by Daya Devi-Doolin.

How would you like to take a dose of a Super Vita-Minds' chapter prescription before you get out of bed in the morning and before you close your eyes in the evening? Allow yourself to be quiet after you drink in the words. Feel the power that they generate within you. Look at the power they will generate in your entire body. Your body will tingle with the Holy Presence when you do so, because you have invited it.

Excerpts from "Super Vita-Minds: How to Stop Saying I Hate You…To Yourself:"

- I breathe in the Peace of God.
- I rest in the Peace of God.
- I live in the Peace of God.
- I love in the Peace of God.
- I sleep in the Peace of God.
- I am willing to and I intend to forgive my (sister, mother, father, the auto mechanic, doctor, surgeon, co-worker, supervisor, son, daughter, cousin, in-law, the rain, hurricane, God, the hit and run driver, minister, murderer, etc).

- I give myself permission to forgive myself for being (weak, non-goal-oriented, unloving, unforgiving, not being there for my friend, my children, my husband, my wife, too fat, too skinny, too lustful, too jealous, too greedy, too selfish, too religious, not religious enough, etc.).

*Choose one statement each day 70 x a day for 7 days and apply it to your life.

Ask yourself, Is ego my father or my Father? I have found for myself that ego is nothing but fear. It is simply a thought system we have mis-created. We have allowed it to separate ourselves from the Prime Creator (the thought of separation itself is an illusion). It keeps us a prisoner or slave to habits and personal thought patterns. It keeps us stuck in day-to-day life situations until we say, "Enough! I surrender all illusions about myself to the Holy Spirit." Ego blocks us from accepting our good because we do not feel we deserve our good or deserve to be loved.

I am the Christ just as Jesus Christ is and so are you. I know and believe we are endowed with the Christ Consciousness just as He is endowed with it. Jesus is perfect. He always chose to listen to the Holy Spirit. He never allowed idols like anxiety, fear, jealousy, condemnation, judgment and fear of lack of money, distrust or dissatisfaction to be His "Father."

We choose these idols to be our "father" and then allow ourselves to be dissatisfied with the manifestation that these choices bring about. These choices keep us in a vicious cycle by choice, and because these choices are so invisible and silent, we dismiss them as being effectual, non-real.

Jesus was the Master of His physical life because He chose to think highly vibrational thoughts that radiated in and without His being. He did it to show us that we too can be the

Master of our lives. He did it to let us know we do not have to crucify ourselves every day with condemning thoughts about ourselves. It is a choice we make, to listen to the voice for ego or the Voice for God, the Holy Spirit.

It has been my personal intention to sit in the seat of receptivity of my highest good. Part of that intention includes having beautiful holy children, a beautiful luxurious place to live, a flourishing metaphysical healing center that touches the lives of others, a fantastic recording career that uplifts thousands and positive uplifting metaphysical books that heal with His Word. I intend to keep sustaining and nurturing the love of myself and developing deep abiding friendships. I intend to write the necessary books, articles and newsletters that I am guided to write. I intend to reach millions of people who are seeking and desiring to change their lives for the better.

My philosophy includes believing that we can make our lives a blessing for all who come in contact with us. Make your intention a powerful one. Make your intention to Love Yourself as powerfully as you can make it. Do everything you can possibly do to have fun while doing this. Let your joy be in the doing for yourself and celebrating yourself. Bless yourself every single day and give thanks always for the beauty within you. My love is with everyone and I hope you will begin to look past illusions from the "outside in" so you can know you are love as well.

When we totally and completely love one's self, there is absolute trust and faith in all your decisions, because you are recognizing the God-Self that you truly are. Your God Self can make no mistakes because you are operating from Love and Love cannot be but loving.

A quote from Marianne Williamson, "The universe is intentional. It is always moving in the direction of greater love, regardless whether or not we consciously align with that love.

When we do align with it, we thrive. And when we do not, we suffer. This is not "punishment." It is merely the Law of Cause and Effect. With each thought we think, we either align with universal love, or we disconnect ourselves from it. Whichever is our choice determines whether we then feel connected to, or disconnected from, our own true Selves."

I have led you to know this so you can experience the many Universal principles and tools you can use at any time and I have incorporated them in my life and in my family's so that we can experience living a healthy, mental and spiritual lifestyle.

We see the *Door of Everything* open itself to us and we walk through the many mansions beyond it that are there for us to explore. You can do the same thing with your pure Intention.

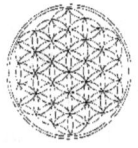

Chapter 2

What is Ego?

What is ego? Ego is fear. It is simply a thought system we have mis-created. It's always a choice we make - to listen to the voice for ego or the Voice for God, the Holy Spirit. Ego's use of guilt, anger, blame, judgment, criticism, etc. keeps us in a prison and what we give out we receive while in that prison. Giving is having and giving is receiving. If we give out judgmental thoughts, critical thoughts or words or deed, that is what we are proclaiming to manifest in our life. That is what we will be receiving. Also, you cannot give what you do not have. You cannot give love if you are not loving and therefore you will not receive it or know that you have truly received it from Christ on a parallel reality.

What you give out comes back to you magnified sometimes a hundredfold and more. We block the channel of good from coming to us because of our disbelief that it could happen. We would be able to see the miracles before our eyes daily if we were willing to change our perception about what we think we see.

If we don't know what we see, we can ask Jesus Christ or the Holy Spirit to reveal the true meaning to us. Instead of seeing ourselves as limited (ego's view of ourselves) and lacking, unhealthy, getting old, weary, unloved, we could turn those thoughts over to the Holy Spirit and begin to see ourselves as totally whole, safe and secure. The vibration of those words alone such as "I am whole, safe and secure", "I am my perfect weight", "I have more than enough money to have fun, travel and serve others" will heal you immediately. The Light energy of those words explodes energy into the dark cells of our being and radiates love everywhere, within and without. It allows us to walk on water (turmoil in your life), as did Jesus.

In seeing beyond ego's vision, we have to be totally GRATEFUL for everything you see around you happening in your life and around you NOW. That's how you change things, by being grateful, not by being critical or judgmental of anything or anyone. Once you are grateful for the space in your consciousness that you have graduated to, you can move into an even more un-limiting consciousness and become more of a servant to mankind on an unconditional level.

Being grateful de-crystallizes all negative energy blocks on a cellular level, emotional/mental and spiritual level within and in the physical realm. When we put ego in its rightful place, which is that of a teacher instead of our Father/Mother God, we will automatically get off the treadmill of "I hate myself, I hate my life, I hate the world." syndrome. We can say thank you ego for letting me know I don't want to be in this space anymore. Thank you for showing me there must be something better for me than this mental, emotional, physically debilitating space that I've mis-created. I am grateful that I can change. I am grateful I have changed and I am grateful I am Master of my Life!

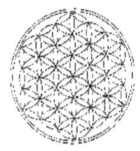

Chapter 3

What Does Sickness Offer You?

Are you sick? Have you ever been sick? What are the payoffs for having been so? I've been sick and I know we get to feel important; people are paying attention to you as you complain, or brag about your condition (i.e. I had double bypass surgery, well I had triple bypass surgery and my scars are thinner than yours).

We get to feel sorry for ourselves for being in pain and incapacitated. If you are sick, you get to hate yourself for not being strong but weak. You get to punish yourself more by playing a guilt trip on yourself. You get to ask yourself Why me? As A Course In Miracles tells us, to obtain what sickness offers, you are willing to attack the Divinity in your brother and lose sight of yours. And you are willing to keep it hidden and to protect the idol of sickness you think will save you from the dangers for which it stands, but do not exist.

When you do not value yourself you become sick, but Christ's value of you can heal you because the value of God's son is One. Peace comes from God through Christ to you. Christ says that, "When a brother is sick, it is because he is not asking for peace and therefore does not know he has it. The acceptance of peace is the denial of illusion and sickness is an illusion.

"Every Son of God has the power to deny illusions anywhere in the Kingdom." Christ can heal us because He knows us. He knows our value for us and He says it is value that makes us whole. Christ will heal you merely because He has only one message, and it is true. Your faith in it will make you Whole when you have faith in Him. I love you.

Nothing can replace God. Whatever attempts we make mean nothing. We may believe we are afraid of nothingness but we are really afraid of nothing. In that awareness are we then healed. In the awareness that I AM Power, that's where I find that Reiki comes into a person's life. When I offer a Reiki session to them, they realize there are no longer any desires in the gods they made to replace God and they want to get in touch again with their divinity, peace and clarity. **Nothing can replace God.**

You will only hear the god you made to listen to. We have made the god of sickness for ourselves and for our children, yet we did not create the god of sickness because he is not the Will of the Father. He is therefore not eternal and will be unmade for you the instant you signify your willingness to accept only the eternal. The eternal truth is you are beyond sickness. You are beyond limiting beliefs.

Ask yourself if killing yourself is what God/Yahweh desires for you? What about cursing your day? Is that what God-Mind would have you do or to gift yourself with the underlying blessings the Universe provides to you? In the spaces that surround you, you are embraced by invisible LIGHT FORCE energy that proves and provides all you need to tap into for your blessings.

It's all our choice which day we want to have. It REALLY is up to us to think a certain way and experience that certain way that we have created! When we stop crying and start smiling and stop sobbing and start living and loving, we won't have time to remain out of the Vortex of blessings. Someone is watching, listening and learning from you one way or the other who you "believe" you are. No one can MAKE you think a certain way even though they may think they know what's best and they may even KNOW what would be for you, but ultimately, you are the ONE who thinks, chooses, writes and films the script. I am adding my blessings to the Light Force energy for all who wish to receive.

Time to practice your I AM Power. Take a moment now to repeat: I am willing Heavenly Father to accept only the eternal in my life. I release my hold on all my illusions. I am willing to totally and completely surrender my will to Yours.

We do not realize how vigilant we are to listen to our gods –god of lust, god of jealousy, hatred, overeating, drinking, drugs, etc. and how vigilant we are in their behalf. Yet they exist only because we honor them.

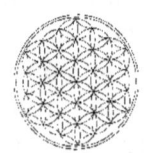

Chapter 4

Practicing the Holy Instant

"Place honor where it is due and peace will be ours. It is our inheritance from our real Father." (ACIM)

There are what I call the Two Cups and they are "I AM" and whatever words we place in those two cups, we reap what we say. We reap what we say, good or bad.

Take a moment now to practice being quiet and repeat, the kind of words you now choose to place in those two cups.

- I am willing Heavenly Father to accept only the eternal in my life. I release my hold on all my illusions. I am willing to totally and completely surrender my will to You. I am willing to forgive myself and trust in You Lord.
- I feel good!
- My mind is good!
- My body feels good.
- My thoughts are pure.
- I love me.
- I love all of me.
- I sleep well each night.
- My mind is happy.

- My abdomen, colon and intestines feel good.
- My income is perfect.
- I now purchase whatever I like without fear.
- My bank account is full of unexpected flow.
- I am a magnet for good from all directions.
- My heart is happy and feels good.
- I let go of all anger.
- I see the good and positive of every situation.

When you apply the Law of Attraction, the Law of Cause and Effect, then conditions change spontaneously. Conditions must change for you.

There is what Dr. Emmet Fox has called the Prescription. It's a 7 Day Mental Diet. It has been very helpful in changing my life for the better. The Prescription calls for us to not allow ourselves to dwell for a single moment on any kind of negative thought about yourself.

- Watch yourself for a whole week as a cat watches a mouse.
- Do not allow your mind to dwell on any thought that is not positive, constructive, optimistic or kind.
- Some extraordinary changes for the better will have come into your life. Start with the assistance of subconscious mind going before you.
- Allow yourself to be free from mental environment of negative speaking people about what they believe you can or cannot do.

What to do when negative thoughts come – turn them away. Say for example, "I am courageous. I am victorious." Brush those negative thoughts away. Do not tell others you are on this path or that you intend to go on it. Keep this tremendous project strictly to yourself. Your soul is the Secret Place of the Most High. Remember, as Dr. Emmet Fox says, "When faced with a troublesome situation that may want you to entertain worry about it, say "None of these things move me." There is no power greater than the Power of God. Use that as your mantra if you wish.

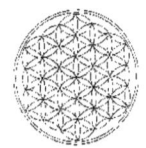

Chapter 5

How to Give Yourself a Spiritual Facelift!

What you will learn if you do this:
1. You will learn how to clear any unwanted negative mental energy, also known as erroneous thinking. There are many levels of consciousness, many levels of awareness and we are given the choice to live in any one we choose. We can reach any one level anytime we choose. We are guided and led by the Voice within our hearts. When we are quiet, we hear that Oneness and feel it and then we become Oneness. We are witnesses to the awesome beauty of it all.
2. Decide it is time to get rid of your old clothing, old articles of the past and throw them away.
3. Think of your old habits, old ways of thinking about yourself as old clothes as not useful anymore because they no longer fit.
4. Decide that abusing yourself is no longer helpful, pleasing or satisfying for you to learn from.
5. Decide that saying, "I am a loser" is no longer able to fit in your new level of awareness. It sticks out like a tear in a new garment.
6. Decide you are going to enjoy life.

7. Decide you will no longer see yourself as imprisoned. This is your life, your choice. You can say I hate you to yourself every day of your life and it will never bring you the joy you know must be "out there".
8. You can also say I deserve to be happy regardless of what I used to believe about myself or what anyone else believes is true about me now.
9. Know I was wrong but I can change my beliefs about myself. I will change my belief. I will absorb positive thought vibrations into my subconscious bloodstream and be uplifted immediately.
10. You can say, "I do accept my Holy-ness." It is my inheritance from the universe. I intend to be happy now because I have decided to do so!

Some positive vibrations to live in your new consciousness level (mansion):

- I give myself permission to forgive myself.
- Everyone loves me. It is their desire to prosper me and to help at any time.
- I love everyone. It is my desire to prosper everyone whom I can when called upon or not.
- My breath is slow and quiet. Peace flows through me like a river.
- All physical problems are dissolved along with my faith in them. I am thankful. You can think of 35 more for your 40-day spiritual facelift and personalize them for yourself!

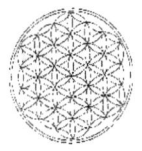

Chapter 6

How to Overcome Depression

Knowing that we are depressed is one of the keys to overcoming depression. Knowing that everything we do involves choice.

Everything is choice. Every decision we make, we choose to make it. We decide what we think and we decide what we think is best for us. We can choose again if the result doesn't feel good or feel right. Thoughts are things and there are no thoughts that are neutral, meaning there are no thoughts that have no effect upon your world. Every thought we have has an effect on us because of its power, energy and vibration. No word we put forth from our mouth returns to us void.

Another key or step is *forgiveness*. Forgiveness is the key that parts the way of the Red Sea of your life. You can forgive yourself by saying "I forgive myself for what I thought I have done. I was mistaken. I apologize to myself. I love myself completely and profusely."

Forgive another by saying, "I forgive you for what I thought you have done to me. I was mistaken. I apologize to you. I release you to your good. I no longer choose to hold you in my mental prison as responsible." If you need to, you can forgive yourself or that person or persons 70 x 7 days until you no longer feel uncomfortable, irritated or depressed when you think of them.

Another step you might decide or choose is to surrender the struggle, the pain, the anguish, the illness, the hopelessness, the unforgiving nature, and the depression and not claim it as yours anymore. We can stop any thought of ours because it is ours, nor anyone else's. Only we can think our thoughts and we can stop any oppressive thought. If it doesn't make us feel good, we can upgrade our thoughts one level at a time to that which makes us feel better emotionally.

You might have a thought like, How do I stop thinking I am unworthy of anyone's love, anyone's companionship or forgiveness? You can program your mind by saying, I can do it by deciding "I am worthy." So, that is what I say and own now, "I am worthy." That is what I claim as the truth for myself. The energy of the words that come forth from you in saying, "I am worthy." puts forth the command to the Universe that you desire something better of life. You will be attracting those aspects of life that prove to you, you are worthy of receiving any desire that is best for you.

The Universe will agree with anything you say and believe as real. All you need do is trust, receive and accept your new life's energy.

Decide to change one habit a week. If you drink 10 sodas a day, choose to drink maybe 2 a day, or 2 every other day, or 2 once a week until you are down to none a day. Soda wears away the enamel of your teeth and irritates the tissue of your colon and intestines, among other things. If you are a shopaholic, for example, go on your shopping spree. Then return everything you bought that day and get money back for a vacation you've wanted to take. Or use the money to give to a charitable organization that arranges to give clothes to people looking for job interview apparel. Or you could tithe the money saved to an organization that you feel helps your spiritual growth.

Look into changing what you are now eating. See if some of the foods could be depleting your energy. See if caffeine, chocolate, artificial ingredients need to be taken out of your nutritional intake. See if artificial sweeteners could be adding undue stress for your nerves, muscles, etc.

If what you are doing is not working, then you must choose to do something different in order to see something different in your life. Claim a new world by claiming, "I have reasons to be happy. I claim happiness and gratitude." The Universe, again, will prove to you that you correct.

And lastly, be grateful. Be grateful where you are in your consciousness now because it is prompting you to know you are in a place that does not make you feel happy. My husband Chris and I were homeless at one time and I would not be where I am today if it were not for my being grateful for everything, friends, churches, books, who I was and for what desires were placed in my heart, my health, etc.

Each level of gratitude I embraced, the Universe doubled it, and gave me back more to be grateful for so now my cup "runneth" over.

Tips:
- Believe and trust in yourself.
- Surrender old thought patterns and accept new healthy ones to Christ, God, The Lord, Universal Mind or Infinite Mind.
- Forgive yourself first and others next.
- Remember thoughts are not neutral, they are things!

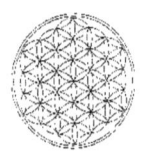

Chapter 7

How to Get What I Want and Not What I Don't Want!

In this chapter, you will learn to focus on what you want and not what you don't want in your life! We begin by knowing that we must focus our energy on what we desire to manifest for us. What we focus on with fear, our subconscious mind matches that fear vibration for us because we have put our energy, feeling, belief and intention behind it and our subconscious mind desires only to focus on manifesting that "thing" we are engaged in thinking upon so strongly. If we focus on what we do want and dismiss what we do not want, our subconscious mind focuses on matching that thought vibration (frequency) with the same amount of dedication and energy to bring to us that which we believe is possible. Former President Obama is a great example of what I'm speaking about.

He didn't allow anyone to make him think or act in any way except to fulfilling his destiny, his goal, his plan to become President. Subconscious mind answered him back with the energy of proving to him that he was right about being the President of the United States. If you want to be disgraced, then you must do something disgraceful in order to render that manifestation to yourself through the help of our genie, our subconscious mind. It does not judge your thoughts as good or bad or unworthy. It honors back to us in matching vibration, that which we believe strongly about, whether erroneous or not.

If you want clients for examples or customers, you are telling your subconscious mind you don't believe you have customers or clients so you get more of lack of clients and customers because that is what you are focusing your thought and belief in.

When you are grateful for customers and clients that you have, your subconscious mind will begin to work things out for you to confirm your belief in customers and clients and their increase because you have begun to be grateful for things unseen first.

If you are in pain, go to the next level of consciousness and start believing all pain has been de-crystallized, dissolved, that the cause has been lifted from your conscious mind and subconscious mind will verify that for you through your belief. You must believe, have faith in and get in the frame of mind by choice and you will receive a new perspective.

If you are out of work, then being in work is what you might want to start holding as the truth for yourself. Telling everyone you are out of work compounds the belief that you are and subconscious mind will work with you to continue making that a truth for you, even though you say you want to work.

Your vibrations are strongly one of being out of work, staying out of work so long as you continue voicing that "truth" which is an untruth. As soon as you begin saying I am in the process of getting a job, then around the corner is a friend of a friend who is hiring your particular qualifications and you find if you had only had belief in the other direction, you might have been working sooner.

Statements like these can help you:
- My vision of a trim and fit body is now in the process of becoming a reality.
- My health is better than ever.
- I am succeeding in areas of my life where I never succeeded before.
- I am on "autopilot"; my body is tireless, filled with energy and power.
- I am a dynamo. My friends look at me in awe as I power through every day with unstoppable confidence and a passion filled drive to succeed at everything I do.
- I am in the process of putting into the bank, hundreds of thousands of dollars through all my avenues of abundant God sources of income.
- I love seeing myself grow spiritually, emotionally and financially. I see all my dreams and goals popping up in rapid manifestation for me like, in days.
- I don't push my dreams away from me with doubt, negativity, disbelief and ungratefulness. I accept them!

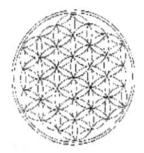

Chapter 8

Did I Really Ask for This?

Do you say, "I want more love in my life?" Do you say, "I want more money to enjoy as I please? "I want a job with higher pay?" Do you say, "I want to get in touch with myself and know who I am intimately?" Do you say, "I want more power, self-esteem, serenity and freedom and to feel liberated, relaxed and comfortable wherever I am?" Do you say, "I want health, abundance and beauty?" Do you say, "I want more life? I want to live?" Do you say, "I want to love myself completely?" In saying, "I want", you are being in a realm, a space of being dissatisfied. You have asked the Universal Law of Mind, by your concentration, faith and belief in your dissatisfaction, to keep on presenting to you exactly what you really don't want but don't believe you are the one keeping you in your undesirable place of consciousness.

Being ungrateful, keeps you unhappy even though you say you desire to be happy. Smile. Believing that you lack health, abundance and beauty aligns you with the illusion with full power and tells the Universe to keep supplying you your truth (personal lie) to yourself so you can know that what you believe in is the truth about yourself.

So you never get up to the mountaintop because you believe in your lack, you make it real by your belief, faith and emotion and it becomes real for you. Universal Mind, Law of Attraction, Subconscious Mind merely aligns your thoughts with similar thought vibrations to make what you believe is real, real.

The Universe honors every thought we have, honors what we believe in strongly, whether right or wrong for you or erroneous. Saying for example, "I want to love myself and be free!" keeps you separated from yourself from the real truth about yourself by believing in your lack of love for yourself.

Turn that around, turn those thoughts around, transmute the energy of that statement to I Love Myself and I AM free and in an instant, you could see that you love yourself and you are free already and have been, but just thought differently about it before.

In the eyes of Creative Source, Infinite Mind, if you will put as much faith and belief in those statements, you will begin to see you do not lack love of self and the Universe will provide the reassuring truths to you daily about your transformed thought, body and mind.

Any time we claim lack in anything (by our faith and belief in that "fact"), the Universe says yes, you are, and I am happy to oblige more lack for you to prove to yourself you are in lack, as you BELIEVE. Any time we claim we are in want, then we shall truly be supplied more want. You put yourself out of the realm of having when you claim you want.

You do not believe you have and so you do not have. Change your words. They are the flesh for you to spring your thoughts into manifestation, action and results. You believe you are outside of your desire, instead of being your desire. Having and claiming you have your desire is now consciousness, living your desire that you had separated yourself from is now as it was from the beginning.

You must discontinue believing in "your" lack. You must discontinue "wanting" because you are saying to your Super-conscious mind, I wish I could but I can't and so it is. The Universe agrees with your thought because thoughts are power, thoughts are things and thoughts are not neutral. The Universe agrees with you on everything YOU believe to be true even though it may not be. The Universe is for you. The Universe backs you up every time. The Law of Cause and Effect is always operating the moment we have a thought.

Author, David Allen has just published a book and it's called, "Askffirmations: Questions that Create Reality". It's using the power of 3 words, "How did I?" He writes, "How did I" gives me the consciousness that the works are done. It is thinking FROM the end. It is using imagination to create reality. When you say the words "How did I" you are giving birth to the impression... and if you maintain the feeling that the works are done, it drops off into your subconscious mind and the subconscious mind brings it to fruition... the expression (the harvest, the condition) that the impression (the image, the seed) your words created. How WONDERFUL is it to KNOW this? "How did I" are 3 powerful words WHEN we know how and why they do what they do. https://amzn.to/2nSo8qy

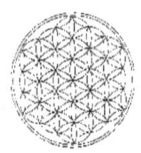

Chapter 9

Creating My Heaven on Earth

When I use the word Heaven, I am referring to our spiritual mind. When I use the word Earth, I am referring to our physical mind, our 3rd Degree dimensional mind.

Creating your Heaven, your peace is using thought patterns and thought forms that can change your life.

There are techniques to free yourself from fearful thoughts. Holding the following words that are most sacred in your consciousness will free you because there can be no place for fear when you do.

Fear will have to take up residence somewhere else. These words are like a mantra in that they have a highly vibrating frequency to them that light up the organs, glands, tissues, cells, aura and spirit.

When we make the statements aloud or silently a couple of times a day, our subconscious mind or deeper mind gets ready to act on the feeling nature behind your intention and lovingly draws unto you exactly what you desire for your highest good.

For example, your affirmation could be:
- The Joy of the Lord (Law) is the strength of me.
- I know it and I claim it now. Freedom and peace of mind belong to me.
- I am changing and ego is dying to Spirit.

- I am transforming into something new and beautiful.
- God is healing me now according to my belief.
- Freedom from alcohol, smoking, jealousy, lustfulness, coveting, overeating, stealing and more exists for me now in the Infinite Mind of God. Each day I grow in understanding of the Supreme Law, which brings freedom forward into manifestation for me.
- I do not try to force anything.
- I let it come forth through my awakening consciousness and I give thanks for it even before my physical eye sees it in form. I give thanks now.
- This is what I know about myself. I am strong, a warrior and I am through being a victim unto myself or to anyone else. I have stepped over into the Realm of Freedom.
- I am blessed to be surrounded by the Light and by the Power of the I AM He. I am in the Presence of the I AM that I AM daily, minute by minute by minute.

As is stated in the Text of A Course in Miracles (ACIM), "What is Fear? Nothing. Nothing unreal exists. What can harm you? Nothing. What is there to fear? There is nothing to fear. There are no neutral thoughts. All thoughts produce after their own kind."

Thought is Energy, Thoughts are things! Thoughts have form that are invisible, but nonetheless have the power to manifest whatever we hold onto strongly in our belief. Thought is substance. Thought is our inherited gift we've been given through our One Source.

When you believe and know that as we've said before:

- "The Holy Spirit is my only invited guest." Then it shall be so.
- When you decide to love, embrace and live, knowing that, then it shall be so.
- "Fear is the stranger here." You will have freed yourself from fearful experiences.

When negative thoughts try to make themselves attractive to you, pull forth from within yourself the vibrational thought:

- "In my defenseless, lies my safety." All quotes used in this section, come from the workbook of (ACIM) used with permission & from *Dabney's Handbook On A Course In Miracles,* Daya Devi-Doolin, Padaran Publications.

"Stop thinking about the difficulty, whatever it is, and think about God instead. This is the complete rule, and if only you will do this, the trouble, whatever it is, will presently disappear." The Golden Key ~ Dr. Emmet Fox

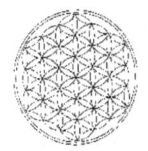

Chapter 10

How to Manifest Total Healing

The moment you say "I surrender my will totally into the hands of the Holy Spirit", your subconscious mind goes to work on making that a reality and you need not ask "HOW?" The how is left up always to the Subconscious Mind or Infinite Mind.

"In the eyes of Infinite Mind, if you will put as much faith and belief in the statement, I AM free, as you do in I AM not free, you will begin to see you are free instantly and in reality, you do not lack for anything." Daya Devi-Doolin

If you are having a difficult time with releasing pounds for example, using an affirmation like this one helps settle the mind, calls upon subconscious mind to come into play and shows you the HOW. Next step is to follow the directions and realizing and repeating the following affirmation with feeling and belief.

"All the food I eat is easily assimilated, digested, eliminated easily and effortlessly."

"I am a child of the absolute good. God is good and I am good. Everything that comes into my life is good and so I am going to have only the good. Only the good is attracted to me and my life is in a perpetual state of joy!"

If you are contemplating a new career, new job, new relationship, new venture, know this:

"I am Master of the vibration that comes out of me and that is the truth! No-thing, nor person can ever change that. If the vibration of my energy is self-pity, powerlessness, hurt, fear or anger then that is what shall be my experience because I have claimed my faith in it. I am the vibration and the vessel of that experience. I choose my vibration and the experience. I choose to be in harmonic resonance with God. I Am One with God."

"I no longer need to feed my ego. I am free. I am free from the chains that once bound me."

In dealing with a disease like arthritis, diabetes or other disease, here are some affirmations and Super Vita-minds' positive thought forms that you can use so you no longer live your life in fear or in pain. These statements can cancel, cancel the energy of fear statements when they are spoken with feeling and intention. Check in within your true self to be sure there are no un-forgiveness issues that need to be cleared between you and another or you and the Universe.

These affirmations are to be said with feeling, belief and trust. The subconscious mind will work on bringing these realities to you in surprising ways because your intent and focus is in a new direction to guide it.

- I AM He. I AM That. (So-hum, yogic mantra)
- I AM that I AM. I AM that which I desire to be.
- God is my strength and power.
- Repeat the name of Jesus Christ as a mantra. The vibrations of the sounds are very healing.
- My body responds to my mind. It is my servant. As I think uplifting thoughts so does my body respond to the life giving energy my Word provides.
- I claim my healing now. It is done.

- Fear does not harbor healing. It cannot.
- I can only be a Host to fear or a Host to the Holy Spirit, but not both at the same time.
- I choose to claim health instead of pain.
- There has to be a better way and I accept it now!
- I live in the realm of health and wholeness.
- Anything I want, health, finances, friendships, career, I speak into existence.
- I always win!
- I am a magnet!

There is a metaphysical technique called "I remember when" that Neville Goddard taught. I have used it in my life. It's pretty simple and I was reminded of it when I entered into the Texas Longhorn restaurant one day to meet friends. Their radio was playing a song called, "Remember When" and a male singer was giving thanks for the memories he and his wife had loved, raising kids and seeing them go off to make their way.

I'll give a few of my examples of its use in a few moments. When you look at the present and are unhappy about what you 'think' you see as real, then use this technique and you will begin building a healthy consciousness or a changed external experience will develop.

I picked up a piece of typing paper that was clean. I got a photo of my husband Chris all dressed in a tuxedo. He had been not too happy with the pounds he had put on. For about 25 of our 40 years of marriage he weighed about 175 lbs. He started to creep to 190-195, 199 and was beginning to get concerned enough to change his eating habits. So with this technique, I wrote on the photo that I had glued beside his photo, "I remember when Chris was not happy with his weight. Now he's back to being trim, healthy and trim and a happy divine being."

So when you use this technique, you change the future while in the present, in the now and you lift your spirit up and start to see there can be a new reality to yourself, physically, mentally and emotionally. You cannot be 'stuck' when you use your words in this manner.

For our finances on the same page, I glued $100 dollar bills (photocopy) in stacks of $10,000 packets. I wrote alongside the photocopy "I remember when we were poor, homeless, broke and in debt. Now – we are abundantly supplied and we know why we are wealthy and debt free because. The reasons are because we've accepted our multiple income and allowed our subconscious mind to work out the kinks and create the vibrational frequency necessary to match our changed view and changed perspective about our finances.

The first day of our marriage, we became homeless for seven months because someone in our band stole our rent money from our hiding place. It was for our rent and small honeymoon trip. By reading Catherine Ponder books for free in the Cambridge, MA metaphysical bookstore, we were able to see our first real income in late fall and move into an unfurnished apartment with no refrigerator. So, I could have written, "I remember when we were homeless, no income, no welfare, no car and no place to sleep out of the rain and cold weather. Now we have a beautiful home with a pool, pets and luxurious cars and multiple income sources."

When you use the "I remember when" technique, you are telling your subconscious mind things are better and better now and you are thankful. Subconscious mind acts on that truth and continues making things better and better for you. This technique takes you from trying to figure out how to MAKE things better. You cannot do this. You do not know HOW. When you leave everything to the creative mind – subconscious mind and imagination - you materialize far more than you could ever know existed for you to be manifested.

One of the other photos on that page was one of me at a lesser weight in leotards, socks and sneakers outside of our resort room. What I wrote was, "I remember when I was not grateful at my weight. But now I am grateful for my progress at releasing weight and eating better. I love you God. I love myself greatly. I love my faith in God and myself for I am a Divine Being."

Here again, you are impressing creative mind with what you know is the real truth even if you don't believe it right away and subconscious mind doesn't know if it's a truth or lie. It only acts on what you believe, what you feel to be true at the time. So why not give it happy thoughts and directions.

Clearing the limiting belief of fear of failure is a great place to begin your journey back to happiness.

You can sing your affirmations, record your voice on audio of your iPhone, write them or repeat them 3-4 times a day. These frequencies will be a gift to your subconscious mind, as you believe while you are doing it. The subconscious mind doesn't discern whether you believe or not in your words or whether you are right or wrong, it just acts on the words, feeling and intent you put into them. "What you focus on strongly, will absolutely materialize for you." Excerpt from Grow Thin While You Sleep – Daya Devi-Doolin

"Faith is to believe what we do not see, and the reward of this faith is to see what we believe." – Saint Augustine.

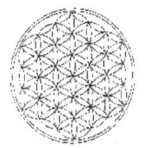

Chapter 11
How to Empower Myself

One of the most important options to consider in empowering oneself is to ask do I need to forgive myself for any wrong-thinking about myself, for having limiting and degrading thoughts about myself, what I look like, how degrading my thoughts are about myself. That is huge isn't it?

But that is what we need to do. Subconscious mind will be the energy force to release this information to you. As I've said before, it doesn't judge good or bad your thinking, but it will put you on the path you desire and choose to "walk" on to experience your manifestation.

Once it's revealed to you from within yourself, you learn how you dis-empowered yourself from knowing and receiving your good by the limiting thoughts you'd chosen to hold onto and mistakenly believed about yourself.

Once you have forgiven yourself or surrendered your wrong-minded thinking to the Holy Spirit, then you are on the way to replacing it with Truth into your consciousness. If you decide there are no illusions about yourself, you will not find your way to the solutions that are already present NOW for you to enjoy.

"When you make an affirmation statement, you are making a positive statement to align yourself with the consciousness of a state of being that already exists for you. You are just remembering this and feeding it into your subconscious, your awareness. You are claiming the truth about yourself. You are not trying to coerce God to change your situation, you are unifying your consciousness with HIS." (Super Vita-Minds: How to Stop Saying I Hate You…To Yourself – Daya Devi-Doolin)

Would you rather say and affirm: "I am sick. I am always sick. Everybody makes me sick" or would you rather say and believe, "I am always well. I always feel good, I live in complete harmony with life" or would you rather say and think "Nothing seems to work for me. The weather is lousy" or "I fully accept all my good or I am happy rain or shine" or "I am always broke or God is my constant supply" or "Everyone always prospers me and I prosper them."

How about asking your Higher Self questions such as put forth by David Allen and Tonya K. Freeman, "How did I know that Prosperity Consciousness, in all forms, would make me feel really, really, really good? How did I know that my life would be so fulfilling, so awesome, so magnificent, so loving? I knew because the God-in-me would have it no other way. Yes indeed." Tonya K. Freeman, Author "Honey Drops" https://www.amazon.com/Honey-Drops-Sweeten-Pot-Life/dp/1973709449.

For financial freedom, you can decide first thing in the morning when you awake to be grateful and thankful for the beautiful and successful day ahead of you. Be thankful for your financial blessings even though they are unknown. Give thanks for the prosperous living in all ways and for that which you are experiencing. You can say aloud, or sing that you are thankful for all the healing aspects of your life. For all the financial joy you are feeling!

Think and Be Rich! One of the very basic keys to understanding about thought is that thoughts are energy. They are substance. They are things and you cannot ignore their power. You must realize there are no neutral thoughts. They travel through timelessness and unlimited boundaries. They are what our beliefs and intentions are composed of.

Utilizing this knowledge, we realize there is no thought we can have that does not have a result or manifestation of that thought. So, if we choose to be poor or rich, that is what will be mirrored back to us because of our belief. Our thought vibration will be matched and we will "sow" the results by our thinking it so. Let us think we are rich and feel that energy and become that energy. Or let us think, we have a harmonious family, harmonious world, harmonious work situation and it shall be according to our belief.

No thought can come into our mind and occupy our attention except when we have chosen to entertain its presence. Everything is choice. No one can put a thought into our mind that we are poor, our vision is bad and our body is ugly, but ourselves. We have to take charge of our thoughts at all times for there are no neutral thoughts as I have already mentioned.

This means that there is no thought we could ever have that would not bring about its causal result. So let's choose to think "I am healthy and whole; I am loving and loveable; I am the best person I can be and I support others in their wholeness in mind, body and spirit."

Being rich is being rich in mind, body and spirit. It's being cooperative, trustworthy and full of integrity, love and forgiveness. We are those things when we believe we are in thought. Let's go to sleep embraced in that energy, wake up in it and give thanks each day and night.

"Thoughts are substance and form. They draw unto themselves the likeness of their own kind." Daya Devi-Doolin

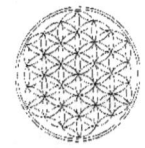

Chapter 12

How to Live the Life I Want

Find your favorite chair and call it your Receptivity Chair from now on. This will be the chair where you will receive your gifts. You will formulate the images of the desires you would have manifested for you and see and feel them manifested right in front of you. You will see the life you want to live right in front of you like magic!

While you are here in your chair, repeat to yourself (your subconscious mind will be eavesdropping), I AM now in the Presence of you Father. I AM now in the Presence of my ideal desire, weight, job, relationship, etc. I AM One with you Father. Thank you for your Love!

"You do not have to beg or plead, convince, struggle or do anything but relax and release old ways of erroneous thoughts and allow God. Be grateful at all times!" (Super Vita-Minds). You might want to write out how grateful you are 1000x. Instead of believing that you are lacking in any one thing, begin believing I have everything I need.

One thing to realize because of its potency in truth, you cannot be deceived if God is with you. And God IS with you. I learned this from A Course in Miracles in no uncertain terms when I started practicing the workbook with Chris.

In the commandment that says, "Thou shall have no other gods before me!" It means do not give power to anything else other than God. Do not separate yourself from the Truth of your being. Do not worship fear, lack, anger, hate, lust or any other types of idols. When you are doing those things, you are giving power to a life of lack instead of one of abundance and power.

In writing this chapter, one early morning around 3:30 am, I was awakened by a loud and soft Spiritual Voice telling me, "What you believe, you become but better yet, what you believe you are, you ARE! You become. You are Spirit. You are what you believe you are. Dwell on that Truth, be that Truth without doubt, confusion or conflict. Your life will change in that instant for the better."

We learn Innocence, as we know it, is pure in behavior and thought. Ego, as we made it, is deceptive – only to preserve itself and keep the truth about yourself from yourself. It "squawks" loudly so as to distract us from hearing the Voice for God, The Holy Spirit.

Perception frees us from questioning as only ego knows how to do. Ego knows only questions because it knows it cannot know the answer. It only knows how to keep you occupied with questions so you won't hear the answers.

A blueprint for Knowing:

- Rise above the ego's voice or lift your mind above ego's voice.
- Look beyond the questions.
- Look beyond illusions.
- Be still – know you are One with yourself, One with Christ.

Affirmations to use.

- Every day I become One with the Word of God.
- I am exhausting limited self and expanding my awareness of my limitlessness.
- Knowledge is always by my side.
- Each minute brings me closer to shedding my ego and replacing it with Knowledge.
- I listen to Your Voice and I am free.
- The puddle I now see will expand into a huge looking glass reflecting back to me the love I see in others.
- A watchful eye always knows that which the ego is trying to hide.

Taking on some of these affirmations that feel right to you will upgrade your consciousness to a new level of joy.

It took me practice to get to that place but I desired it and so it was given. I enjoy holding hands, as we all do, with each other in giving support and standing in that special place – called Love.

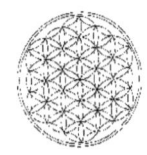

Chapter 13

How Do I Access My I AM POWER?

You will find if you start giving yourself permission to love yourself instead of disparaging yourself, that is the beginning of how to access your I AM Power. By going deep while sitting in your chair of Receptivity and allowing yourself to breathe deeply, repeat these statements until you feel the power of the words. Once you feel a "click" yeah, that is true, move onto the next affirmation and repeat that one until you feel "done".

- I give myself permission not to use my body as a battleground any longer.
- I have no reason to hate myself any longer.
- I have no reason to punish myself any more.
- I give myself permission to be loveable to myself.
- I give myself permission to do fun things.
- I sow loving thoughts to my body, mind and spirit.
- I love my hair, my face, my mind, my body, my skin, my arms, my thighs, my husband, my wife, my sisters, etc.
- I listen to my Comforter (the Holy Spirit) on what to say, think and feel at all times.
- I no longer deny that I hear the Comforter.

- I no longer feel dissatisfied with myself.
- I was mistaken.
- I no longer need to feel dissatisfied with my life.
- I no longer need to drown myself in despair.
- I can no longer not listen to the Holy Spirit.
- I am at One with my health, weight and wealth.
- I no longer need to overeat, to smoke, lust, be jealous and idolize money, sex, clothes, people and other things.
- I am at peace.
- I am still.
- I am not alone.
- I am strong in the Lord (Law).
- All is well!
- I am enfolded by the Spirit of Truth at all times!
- I am forgiven and I forgive myself for believing I was weak and unworthy of LOVE.

You can get your I AM Power back now by writing down or saying aloud, I now decide to forgive because I desire to know peace, freedom, oneness, joy and love. I desire to be free from the pain of un-forgiveness.

Answer the question: what would happen to me if I decided to forgive the government, the president, the boss of my company, my relative(s), my job, etc? What would happen to me? How would I feel?

The answer to move you into your I AM Power would be, I now choose to forgive _____ because I would like to be forgiven and freed from this imagined prison I have built around myself and the person I would forgive. Forgiving them means that I _____.

- "I am a spiritual being bestowed with great power. I am stronger than any doubt from within or any judgment from without." Daily Word a Unity Publication 2018
- "I have the power to conquer any self-limiting thoughts that might otherwise hold me back." Daily Word a Unity Publication 2018
- "I perceive a new possibility and make it a reality through my creative power." Daily Word a Unity Publication 2018

Repeat to yourself aloud – I invite thoughts of happiness, joy, love, peace, truth, calmness, abundance etc. and my mind is closed to anything but these like qualities because I have invited the Holy Spirit to take the place of anything unlike TRUTH and unlike LOVE.

You must stop using the word TRY or TRYING, that doesn't cut it. We either do or not do, it's all a choice. What kind of thoughts make you happy and what kind of thoughts do not make you happy and joyful is your choice to find out. Decide TODAY that using try is not in your vocabulary any longer.

Replace negative thought forms with "The Holy Spirit is my ONLY INVITED GUEST TODAY!" Period. If you let your guard down, then it's a matter of repeating these powerfully vibrational thought forms and finally your subconscious mind will get the direction to help you select those words that are healing to your mind, body and spirit.

Go to sleep with these words, "I rest in the Peace of God. I sleep in the Peace of God." and the vibration of these words as well will be honored by your subconscious mind. There is no hoping, wishing, or fearing, there is only KNOWING that these words are truth for your spirit.

And This Is So at the end of your words before going to sleep. AND if you must say these words again until you KNOW you mean it, then do it over and over and over again until you believe and feel it tingle in your bones. You are the POWER over your life, your THOUGHTS and only you.

Just Do - NOT TRY

For your financial increase and abundance, repeat the words, "Hello money energy. It's a pleasure to count you. I love counting money. I love counting lots and lots of money. We do great things together. I circulate you in shops, stores, people and other ways."

- Use a pillar candle with green color. Draw a $ sign into the candle with a quarter. Put the above intention in the candle as you use peppermint oil and rub the oil all around the candle. Anoint the candle with your belief.
- Write the amount of $7,000 or more or less on a piece of typing paper and fold into three's. Then take it and fold into three again so it forms a small envelope.
- Place the quarter into the small envelop.
- Take the wax from the lit candle and seal the envelope with the quarter inside of it and seal the quarter inside. Say your incantation "Money, I thank you for coming to me" or your own incantation and FEEL it very fast.
- Do this every morning by lighting the candle and forget about the intention.
- Be in gratitude every day and watch it flow silently and quickly into your hands!

Whatever your intention is - it doesn't matter to your subconscious mind because it doesn't judge, it just acts on behalf of our thoughts, beliefs and feelings. The candle and fire are tools that are visual and makes things more concrete. Yes!!!

When you feel it, your mind is closed off to any thoughts, unlike the Christ Light that is within you. The Mouth of God is the Mind of Man - so your word is God's word and nothing has any power over that TRUTH.

Now is the time to give yourself the I AM POWER test. On Facebook there is a group involved in Askffirmations. This story was shared about the group's meaning by authors David Allen and Tonya K. Freeman. She reports, "One of my metaphysical friends asks himself questions that are affirmations or, as a group calls them, Askffirmations. I like that. No, I LOVE that! What are you talking about Tonya? Well, ask yourself this question. How did I know that I was going to be financially wealthy? How did I know that I was going to be loved by a wonderful partner? How did I know that my thoughts would create such an awesome lifestyle? Got the picture?"

An example of how I used my I AM POWER or my CHRIST POWER is when I had a tumor the size of a small pea under the skin of the right buttock. It just showed up one day. I asked how could it be dissolved? The answer came quite quickly and that I was to get in touch with the energy flow of it, the frequency vibrations and declare I am Christ. You can tell the cells to be removed as the Christ. You can demand they go back to the No-Thingness they came from.

So as I lay in bed, I declared the statement as true, with feeling and knowing, and in about five minutes it was dislodged. So I was told by Spirit I can use the same formula for healing my vision or anything else that had concerned me. I've been wearing glasses since I was 2 yrs old after surgery for my eyes being crossed. I was told by Spirit some 40 yrs ago very strongly that I can see. But I have believed my ego and so it has been as I believed. As doctors told me and as my mother told me.

End your day with positive affirmations: I AM BLESSED! I AM a MILLIONAIRE! Say it loud and with love and power!!! You can also end you day saying to yourself, I FEEL LUXURIOUS! I don't know HOW we have been blessed to live such a luxurious life, I only know that we have and that we do and we are truly grateful.

Again, test your I AM POWER within you and be done with all lack, weakness, pain and suffering finally. You ARE the POWER!

I AM CHRIST POWER! I AM THAT I AM! I AM HE and I can do any and ALL things!

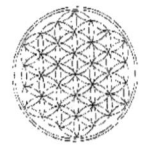

Chapter 14

God's Prescription For Me is Perfect Health & Wealth

Tune into what God's healing prescription is for you and you will find the best natural supplements there waiting for you to be absorbed into your molecules through your breath and mind. It's quite brilliant to find out that His words and the breath are what can turn our lives around from worst to best.

The Universe is constantly offering an ebb and flow of Light energy that transmutes all debris and toxins we are willing to release and let go. Sometimes, even though we don't know we have to release and let go, it decides what needs to be let go and guides us to do so by the people we meet, the book we may have forgotten we read and it turns up for us with a certain page tagged relating to a problem you wanted to solve, etc.

I recall seeing a show that Dr. Oz shared with the public, a show on the techniques for alternative healing which included Reiki and alternate nostril breathing, in Sanskrit Anuloma Viloma. I teach Hatha Yoga and have done so for 50 years. This is a part of the teachings, using the breath for healing.

Alternate nostril breathing is for balancing the left and right sides of the brain. The left side of the brain is for logical thinking and the right side is for creativity.

The optimum benefit of creativity is enhanced and the left side is improved with logical thinking by alternate nostril breathing. It is not the only breathing technique used in yoga for this type of benefit. There is a yogic position for applying this technique called the Vishnu Mudra. You can sit on the floor or a chair if that is more comfortable. In this mudra you use your right hand, touch the thumb, the ring and little finger together http://www.abc-of-yoga.com/pranayama/basic/viloma.asp. You place your left hand, palm up on your lap or knee.

1. There is a breathing rhythm or ratio that is used which you breathe in through the right nostril and count to 2, hold the inhale 8 counts with ring and little fingers closing the left nostril and exhale through left nostril to count of 4 (2:8:4) or

2. Do the inhale to the count of 4 through the right nostril then close with the right thumb.

3. Hold the breath closing both nostrils (the ring and little finger closes the left nostril). Hold the breath for 16 counts.

4. Exhale through left nostril by lifting ring and little finger and count to 8 as you exhale.

5. Repeat by breathing through other side.

You may continue this round of breathing for as long as you like but to start with, maybe three (3) rounds.

The benefits of Anuloma Viloma lead to a calmer mind, a happier disposition, more clarity, more oxygen to the brain cells which benefits the entire body and more logical thinking. You give yourself more I AM Power when you allow yourself to know that you are taking control of your life, your well-being, your health. http://www.home.comcast.net/-bgajjar/index.html.

"Breathing is the bridge between the mind and body therefore Pranayama, with the help of the mind, reduces bodily stress. This technique slows the pulse by teaching the heart to take more oxygen in a shorter time. This technique helps control anger also." -Professor Yogi Bharat Gajjar, http://www.home.comcast.net/-bgajjar/index.html.

I want to remind you that you have permission to change your life through making wiser choices, and allowing changes for the better, in your experiences and for your families. Using the breath as a healing tool is a wise way of using God's prescription for health.

. Many, many years ago, I gave myself time to ask some questions of myself (Higher Presence) regarding my success. Here are some of the questions I asked. Then I answered or filled in the blanks below. The answers are within you as well as within me. The truthful answers, that is. There may be some possible reasons you are not and won't be a success because you might hold these beliefs as truths for yourself:

- I can't believe it is possible for me to….fill in the blank
- I don't have………..fill in the blank.
- I keep saying I wish……
- I have to wait for my kids to …..
- I have to wait until I lose weight before I can…..
- My boss doesn't…….
- I don't have the right clothes to…..
- I don't know how to …….

Ego has a subtle and immature way of dealing with our success or lack of it. Ego wants to keep us in a blame mode outside of ourselves. That way, we won't look at the truth inside of us and solve what we think is our problem.

Repeating the words above or other limiting statements with feeling, belief or emotion cannot benefit you. They cannot assist you in your leap to the next dimension in consciousness. You will continue to experience your thought life through your thought experience until you decide to change the thinking paradigm or thought pattern.

I realized through Spirit that my idea is conceived first in Mind and then in actualization. I know now in consciousness what the truth is for me. I know it shall be and so I allow it to be so. I release it and act as if it already is. It shall be for you the reader as well.

You can be a success at whatever you decide to do just like I have. When we make our decision with our God Self, the God Doer, our creation becomes flawless. If our intention for success is pure, then it will benefit others in the invisible and visible realm. You will be given the ideas to act on until such time as your dream has pushed through the ethers and given birth to itself. It just needs your help in the delivery room by being there and being ready to cradle it and protect it and act on it. It doesn't matter if someone says otherwise about your route to success. What you know about your success ideas is what is true.

When you immerse yourself in communicating with your Self, your I Am Presence, your Higher Self, you make your effort in obtaining your desire effortless. All you have to do is invoke the assistance of our great Helper, our Universal Life Force, God. Our role then is to accept and know it is done unto us.

The Secret of being a success, from Prentice Mulford, author of *Your Life Forces*, "If, then, you think, or keep most in mind, the mere thought of determination, hope, cheerfulness, strength, force, power, justice, gentleness, order and precision, you will attract and receive more and more of such thought-elements. These are among the elements of success. These qualities of thought-element are as real things as any we see or feel. The more you set the magnet in this direction, the stronger it grows to attract these elements." Find out right away which one of these qualities above are missing links or that which may be keeping you out of the realm of success, according to your beliefs. The Universe honors every thought you have. It honors what we believe in strongly, whether right or wrong for us.

Though these qualities are invisible, they are still things. They are thought forms, a force which makes you very powerful in a quiet and gentle and unassuming way. The secret here is that you can only obtain this energy by giving up what does not serve you in this capacity and by magnetizing that which you do want to align with. (Permission granted to use excerpt from Prentiss Mulford's book).

Do you have any forgiveness issues? If you have a burning hatred inside your heart and mind right now and desire to be free of this debilitating energy form, then take the next few minutes to sit quietly and take several deep breaths through the mouth. I suggest to my clients that this will allow God to work through their emotional chakra center (throat) through the breath. I have them do the following steps:

- Bring this person in mind, this condition or thing to mind after they take several deep breaths.
- With their eyes closed, they look into the other's eyes without any fear or hatred on their part.

- I have them see or sense what they are trying to tell them through their eyes or Presence.
- They must listen closely with their heart.
- Breathe with them. Ask them for forgiveness for holding hatred towards them.
- Tell them you release them and let them go through the Grace of God – even if that person is deceased.

One time a female client of mine held sadness for 34 yrs because her mother in-law had committed suicide and never came to her for help so she could have had a chance to prevent it. She never forgave herself until 2 weeks ago in my center. She never realized her physical condition was due to the invisible thought form she was carrying within her heart and liver for all those years.

You can still be forgiven when and after talking with the Higher Presence of someone deceased. Thank God for allowing this healing to take place over time and space easily and effortlessly. You will be and feel so relieved and free as if a surgical procedure had just occurred for you, but it will be pain-free and drug free.

Another way to accomplish this same thing for your health is to:
- Write out your thoughts on a page or in a journal book.
- Write each day for seven days, seventy times each day, "I forgive you (name of person, condition or thing) for your wrong doing" as you saw it or their wrong doing as you saw it.
- Your Word is substance for you to spring your thoughts into manifestation, action and results.

- You must decide to discontinue believing in lack, if you wish to change your outer world.

Does clearing away clutter make a way for what you do want? You bet. When you decide you want fresh clean energy into your aura, into your mind, into your spirit, you must clear away the energy thought forms that aren't bringing the good you desire into your experience. You are what you think and there's no getting around it. "As a man thinks, so is he." – James Allen.

When you think lack and poverty, you believe it and so you prove it to yourself. When you think abundance, you are abundance, believe abundance, that's what the Universe goes about proving to you and presents to you. It also lovingly goes about proving to you your belief about being in lack as well are true. That is the way Universal Law works. The Universal Law about Gravity always works the same every second, every day every year. The Universal Law about the Cause and Effect and the Law of Attraction works in the same way.

So, if you want a change in your spiritual, mental environment, your career environment or relationships, you must make way for it by clearing away the spiritual and mental garbage of toxic thoughts and the Universe will, of course, come to your aid. You just decide with joy to release debilitating thoughts, negative thoughts, thoughts that take you away from your true purpose, your passion, and the vacuum left allows peace, joy, bliss, clarity and freedom to take their places.

Is selfishness tolerated by the Universe? Selfishness is not tolerated and cannot be tolerated and is not even recognized actually by the Universe. Energy just ebbs and flows like the ocean. Change is constant and when we try to hold onto and not allow anything in, our fingers are peeled open the hard way, sometimes developing into sickness, illness, unexpected separation, etc.

The more regularly you tithe for example, the more the Universe, Father Mother God Principle will pour out its abundance upon you. It's because you believe there is no limit to what you can receive. For instance, I can tithe 1/10 of my love, if that is what I need more of. I can tithe 1/10 of my time and that's what I will receive more of. When I tithe 1/10 or more of my prosperity, I will receive that and more from the Universe. If you are holding your hand in a tight, clenched fist to keep your money from flowing out, you receive nothing because your hands are clenched and will not open willingly. You will just exist with money problems, struggling most of your life and wondering why.

When we tithe, we are agreeing that we are willing to believe and trust that more will be given unto us and that nothing will be taken from us as we give. As we give, so are we giving unto ourselves. Once you realize that you lose nothing by trusting, you shall be provided for at all times and be aware of that and give thanks.

How do you think you can you prove it's easy for you to demonstrate money and that it is easily attracted to you?

Take this question to heart, meaning believe and know:
- I am cleaning out the closets of my mind of all negativity.
- I am surrendering my consciousness of lack.
- Money is the easiest thing for me to demonstrate.

- I love my creditors and I love myself for having creditors.
- I know and believe that Light and Prosperity envelop me and my creditors.
- My creditors and I are in a win-win situation now.
- I lovingly pay as I receive.
- I bless the Universe as it unveils ways and means for me to witness abundant living.
- My mailbox is a recipient of Divine Love and I affirm it brings only prosperity and it overflows with money, love letters of all kinds from the entire globe.
- I forgive myself for all the negative thoughts I've had towards my creditors and people who have owed me money.

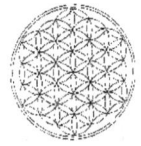

Chapter 15

Our Universal Cellphone

Sometimes I call our connection to the Vortex, our Source of All there is, my connection to our Universal iPhone. Even before Chris and I got married, we felt led to pray before we were leaving for anywhere or before we got into our car for any outing. By doing so, we avoided any undue problems or serious problems. We knew we were in touch with our invisible Angels of protection and still are.

When you remind yourself you are protected, you hear things to do before anything happens, you get warning signs if you listen closely. We have many instances in our lives where we were "warned" about pre-imminent danger and so knew what to do about seeking protection and how to react.

Our family likes taking nature walks and taking small trips. When my youngest son Joseph was four years old, we took him for what "I" thought was going to be a short hike for us. My husband took us to a state park for one of these short trips and when we got there, on the board before entry, there was a very short trail pictured on the map. He said no problem, he knew what we were about to do and that it would not be long. This was about two or three in the afternoon.

There were cow and manure piles we had to step around, over and beyond to get through to our trail. Fine and good. Joseph kept up with us with his little legs. He was excited. I am not a hiker's hiker. I just walk and look for a bench after a while, sit and then move on again. Chris saw trees painted with a blue patch of paint on them – said he knew where we were going because of these. The whole trip was supposed to be less than thirty minutes (there and back).

We kept walking, walking, walking and saw no signs for the turnaround point. We continued walking, walking and walking some more. Tried to make an interesting game of being hunters for Joseph's sake (and mine). We came to a deep pool of mud because it had poured down rain two days before our trip there. Just before getting to it, we had come across a slithering thing in the middle of our dirt path. It stopped right in front of all three of us. It was startled and so were we. It was the same color as the sandy path we were on. We told it that it was safe for it to move on and it did. We watched it saunter along without fear from us harming it. It was some type of snake. No rattle.

Our next adventure was to find a way around that deep puddle of mud. It wasn't easy to be completely free of getting wet and dirty but we did it because we had to.

Two hours pass, not just thirty minutes. We were still in the woods trying to find our way out! We did not have cellphones back in the "olden days" of 1997. We didn't have water or food to drink or eat. Joseph at four years had already become thirsty and hungry an hour or more ago. We had nothing to give him! We didn't see any signs for getting out of the woods. Now the sky was definitely beginning to get darker.

Chris and I always pray before going anywhere from our home as I said earlier and so we didn't know how we would be rescued from this situation, but we knew we'd find a way or it would be shown to us. We weren't exactly scared, not yet anyway. But we were tired, tired and tired, thirsty and hungry just like Joseph. He was getting too tired to walk and since he was not a baby anymore, holding him for long periods of time was tiring for each of us. So we had to figure out how to keep moving to get out of there before dark and keep his weight from slowing us down.

We decided we had to carry him between us. I had my arms and hands under his armpits and Chris had his feet and legs. Then we'd switch positions with him. Can you imagine being young like that and trusting your parents to take care of you? He didn't complain and he didn't hear us complaining. I don't recall him crying either. He just kept trusting as well.

As the sun started to go down, I saw the sunlight reflecting off something tin-like up over our heads and way off in the distance through the woods. I said to Chris that has to be the roof of a house. What else could it be? I said, "Let's walk towards that reflective light." As we got closer and closer, and it must have a mile away from where we first saw it, we could see I was right. We started seeing the top part of a small house. I remember what it looked like to this day. When we got to the house, we walked up the steps of the house and we were about to knock on the door to see if we could get some help or some direction.

We had no idea if anybody would be there because it looked so old. The door opened suddenly and the guy who came out was as startled as we were – only we were startled and happy to see him, anyone!

It turned out he was a park ranger and if we had come five minutes later, he'd have been gone to patrol the park and we wouldn't have been rescued. We told him of our predicament of getting lost and asked him for help. He went around the back of the house and got a Jeep. He said he would drive us out to the exit.

We put Joseph across our two laps, sat in the back seat of the jeep for two people and he drove us out to the exit of the woods. We were so thankful. We were relieved and shaken up at the same time. Chris promised never to take it upon himself to "think" he knew where he was going again when we were with him. He apologized for getting us lost.

All the while we were trudging along through the woods we were being led to this house with the reflective tin roof though we didn't know we were being led there. We just kept trusting on the phone service being given to us from on High. Our Universal cellphone did not run out of batteries. The Universal cellphone we used didn't get stalled or closed down or burned out or come with message, "You are out of service area – bleep". I am grateful we always pray before leaving the house or going on any trips, short or long. I am always grateful for the Universal cellphone we carry with us all the time. It's always dependable and always charged up.

If you happen to find yourself in a difficult situation, remember you are not alone. Remember to trust that you are in good hands and all will work out for the best. There are affirmations you can call forth that live within your God-Mind like I feel good; I feel courageous; I know all is well; I am strong; I am happy, etc.

There is a term called Switchwords which were first identified by Freud and then researched by James T. Mangan in the 1960s. These power words speak directly to our subconscious mind, helping clear blocks to success and activating our ability to manifest love, money, creativity, self-healing and success. Switchwords work, because the subconscious mind actually directs up to 95% of our actions and decisions. For example, if we can't lose weight, it's often because we unknowingly sabotage our efforts due to old belief patterns. If we can't attract money, deep down we may think we're not worth it. Switchwords help clear this negative debris from our subconscious so we can make positive CHANGE in our lives. All you need do is say the Switchwords you need, right NOW. With affirmations and askffirmations, you state the sentences in the present essentially with intention and feeling.

With switchwords, you don't need a sentence, just words or numbers and a space to relate to a particular solution to a problem and your intent. Some examples of switchwords are: Find, star, wow, ridiculous, shine, count, and you can group them together with a space in between.

Here are other words that are believed to work for 95-100 percent of people:

ACT to be a good speaker
ADD to increase; to boost what you have
ADJUST to deal with an unpleasant situation effectively; to deal with a responsibility or burden
ALONE to heal a scab; generally, to promote healing
AROUND for better perspective
ATTENTION to pay attention to detail; to avoid careless mistakes
BETWEEN to discover or boost psychic ability, enhance telepathy
BE to have good health; to be resilient to ridicule and other negative attitudes; to feel less alone; for peace of mind; to do well at sport
BLUFF to reduce or dispel anxiety, fear or nervousness
CANCEL to dispel worry, poverty, debt, annoyance and negativity; any unwanted condition
CARE to remember; retain information
CHANGE to get rid of pain in any part of the body, or anything else unwanted, such as negative thoughts; also to get something out of the eye

CHUCKLE for personal confidence; to turn on personality
CLASSIC to appear cultured
CONTINUE to increase endurance; also, to swim
CONSIDER to be a good mechanic; to diagnose
COPY to have good taste; also, to boost fertility
COUNT to make money; to cut down smoking
COVER to subdue excitement; calm nerves
CROWD to get your children to follow orders
CURVE to make beautiful; to create an item of beauty; also, for self-esteem

There are switchword prescriptions for career/money/health and wealth, etc. Switchwords' link is courtesy of http://switchwordspower.com/switchwords-list/

Always be mindful of your thoughts, feelings and intention as we did on our walk in the woods. We never gave up, that wasn't an option. We kept listening to Spirit to lead us all to safety and we didn't entertain doubt, anxiety or worry.

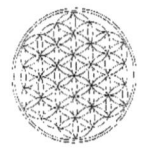

Chapter 16

Freeze Negative Energy

When we want a demonstration, or a manifestation to appear as the result of our prayer and faith, all we have to do is be still and not allow anything to move us from that place of faith. That means we trust, believe in the unseen and know our prayer has BEEN answered – we have to Believe. We are given steps to take on faith and we must listen, act and receive.

What do you want to see manifest for yourself? What do you dream of seeing dissolved or erased or fulfilled?

Here is an example of how we turned around a serious negative event presented in our lives and what we did with our I AM Power.

Friday, February 19, 2011 Chris and I went to bed at 11 pm. We left my oldest son Tyler up watching a DVD out in the living room. Before I went to bed I asked Ty to put the newspapers in the recycle bin outside. It's between our house and our neighbor on a strip of property about 8 feet wide before the neighbor's yard begins.

At 5 am, our phone in the bedroom began ringing. I can hear before answering it by the tone of the energy in the ring, something's not right. I answer it and there is a robotic message that someone in the Volusia County Jail wants to make a collect call named Tyler. We had left Ty in the living room at 11 pm. How could he be in jail? Message was if you wanted to pay for the collect call you had to pay by credit card. Where is your credit card at 5 am in the morning? So we missed out in finding out what happened to him and why he'd be in jail.

Chris figured out how to reach the jail and we found out through jail officials Ty had been arrested for attempted burglary of the next door neighbor.

They kept Ty in jail from 2 am until 2 pm that afternoon even though we paid bail for him to be out sooner. We waited at the jail for him to be released from 8:30 am until 2 pm Saturday.

Ty explained to the police and to us that he wanted to get a snack for his movie and decided to walk 1½ blocks to the Circle K Store. He never got to the store because the neighbor (who happens to be white) called the police on him as attempting to crawl through her bedroom window taking out the screen in the window and then said she saw him running away. The police picked him up before he could enter the store and read him his rights and asked him questions about the supposed burglary. Ty was stunned to say the least. They told him he was lying and didn't believe him.

He told the police as he put out the papers in our recycle bin, the Huskie dog who sits in the window all the time barking, caused the neighbor's roommate to come to the door because of the loud barking. She saw the screen down on the ground and saw Ty walking across her property (about 1/8 on her property) coming down the path I told you about earlier from our two houses to make a short cut to the store. Ty is black by the way, and "witness" told police it was a black male she saw trying to enter the window. We have maintained that the dog being so large probably pushed the screen with its nose trying to get at Ty as he walked from our yard to the street. We have lived in this neighborhood for eight years. They moved in at Christmastime. Ty has lived with us for one year and a half.

Ty never walks anywhere – why? because he has callouses on his feet so thick and painful that it hurts to walk or stand for any long period of time. When he goes grocery shopping, he uses a motorized cart that Wal-Mart has for their customers. He sees a podiatrist, a medical doctor at the VA clinic to dissolve the problem and help get strength back so he can work again. He has not worked in over a year and a half because of this foot problem. He lives with us until he can take care of himself again. So he certainly couldn't and didn't run and he has medical records and x-rays that prove he cannot walk briskly and running is out of the question. He's been getting medical treatment for a year and a half.

The witness told police she saw him running away from the house. There were no fingerprints of his or proof that he was even near their house because he wasn't. She is a drug addict for a fact and she must have been hallucinating about what she saw. There were two ladies who roomed together and two dogs.

We went through interviewing who could and would and who we would want as a lawyer to represent him. We found the best after 10-15 interviews with various lawyers. We did not want a public defender (my husband, Ty and I).

On February 28, 2011 I was led to write this letter to God, placed it in the freezer compartment under the ice tray and my intention was to freeze any action of jail incarceration, to stay any accusations against him, to have all charges frozen and dropped against him. These are the words I wrote down with feeling, belief, emotion and expectation: As of this day, Chris and I are exonerated from being Ty's financial source – We now see him as capable to financially take care of himself thoroughly, completely and I forgive him. His arrest is my gift to myself and a gift to Chris, Joseph and Ty himself to see where we have been holding Ty hostage as dependent upon us. I now allow Ty to choose an alternative for himself. I now KNOW and BELIVE he can handle this case very well to see himself freed, exonerated and independent with no police record. This has opened up an opportunity for him to figure out how to dig himself out of his apparent hole in the ground. I see him with his own apartment, the means to pay for the apartment, the means to have plenty of food where his refrigerator is "stuffed" with good things to prepare and eat.

    The right people (as I write who they are below) are here to help him gather all documents needed to clear his name in court where he will be set free. His eyes are opened to his strength and power. There are more gifts in this scenario ready to be share with all of us. I allow the gifts to show themselves to me now. I demand the gifts to show themselves to all of us!!! I am released from caring for him knowing I can continue to love him without having him be dependent on Chris and I. He sees himself as successful and we see him thusly.

    The Love of Christ Jesus, the Love of Universal Mind, All the Ascended Masters and Beings who work, guide and love us Seal and Bind this Intention Permanently on Earth, my mind and in Heaven and So It Is! Then I signed it.

    I wrote and left this in the freezer without re-reading it or agonizing over whether my prayer would be answered. I released it. Then I was told to call several friends whom I know are very powerful with visualization, intentions, manifesting change for the better. They are Debbie Moran, Felicia Benzo, Inez Bracy, Dr. Nalani Valentine, Mari Leisen, Jeany Perez, Bob and Iris Reynolds plus Chris and me and two other ladies I had just met. We formed a Master Mind Prayer Group of Freedom for Ty. We all aligned with the Truth about the situation and set it aside for the Universe to work out its manifestation plan for him.

One month later in March, Ty and I were coming home from the VA clinic. As I got out on my passenger side, Spirit had my eyes go over the house next door. I saw the screen had been pushed out of the window, hanging by a thread. I said "Ty quick, get a picture of that screen and the dog". We were blessed in another way also as there were no cars outside in the driveway. We tried the camera on my cell phone but the sun was too bright to really get it. So we quickly ran inside, got my husband's camera – and took photos as proof that the dog was the only one who could have done that while owner was gone. Not only that, a FedEx truck and driver had been there to leave a package for me. She told us she would be glad to be a witness to what we all were looking at. We told her of the situation and she was glad to leave name, phone number of how to reach her. We gave all that information to the lawyer and he told us good work. When we saw the screen window out, we praised God. There was no way you could have planned something like that as proof of Ty's innocence and how the screen had gotten pushed out.

  Saturday, April 23rd – I first had my meditation time before jumping out of bed. Then I looked in my mind at the paper I had placed in the freezer with my prayer on it. I had aligned with God in knowing Ty would be exonerated from being accused of the February 19th burglary of the next door neighbor's house. The ANSWER to me was no, no need. Everything's taken care of.

  On this day, I received a forwarded email from one of the powerful women of the Master Mind group and I read it. I followed the directions blindly knowing my friend Debbie doesn't send junk in her emails. She said her father had sent it to her. The bottom part of the forward said your prayer would be granted one way or the other through someone, a phone call, message, TV or some way. You had to put the time you responded to the forward and the date. Love, ME

One hour later the most amazing thing happened that could not have even been planned out that way by another human.

As I was going off with my youngest son Joseph in my car, the neighbors from across the street came waving and running over to me. They have never done that and they only just started speaking to us about two months ago. The wife said the woman next door to you told us today, she's dropping the case against Ty (though he was arrested February 19th) based on her roommate in the house. She said the roommate moved out (moved out based on what I know about the energy and power of prayer) and she had been the one pressing on with accusing him. Well the owner of the house will go to her lawyer on Monday and drop the proceedings against Ty. She told our neighbors across the street she didn't want to have bad feelings going on between her neighbors (us) and herself.

I cried with joy and hugged the woman and her husband. I squeezed her so hard and cried and laughed again and squeezed again so hard as I was trying to tell them I had just heard not to be concerned about praying, or reading my prayer which I kept on paper in the freezer. I cried and they laughed and we hugged some more and husband did a powerful high five with me.

I explained Spirit had already told me. They didn't get it until I said God told me the news that they had just confirmed for me. They were the messengers the bottom part of the forwarded email had referred to and said I would experience.

I wrote to my friends: "Thank you Debbie, thank your Dad and thank you everyone for making this Master Mind Group for Ty and our family manifest the TRUTH. Thank you for the POWER you all exude through your Faith. That's why I called you all forth because your LOVE is so strong!!!!!"

    I felt God Smile and say to me, "Happy Mother's Day Daya."

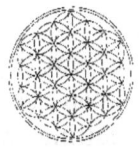

Chapter 17

True Visualization
Using Your Body as a Dowsing Tool

In travelling to cities in France, Italy and Spain recently, for the first time I found one thing was common and necessary in my book, but not for the citizens of these cities. It was finding a bathroom, to me, and water closet or toilet to them. The seemingly necessary thing was unimportant to the tour guides we had. They were far apart during our travel and not given a second thought as to how important they were to this traveler and others. In the spring of April 2016, I was asked to be a Presenter at the Ozark Research Institute on The Top 10 Yoga asanas for alleviating chronic pain. It was an Alternative Healing and Dowsing Conference held in Fayetteville, Arkansas.

I knew a little about Dowsing and learned a lot by the time I left the conference several days later. I learned that my body is a dowsing tool and I can use it as such with my fingers, my subconscious mind and letting myself as a whole be led to be where I was being attracted to be. For instance, I can place my index finger and middle finger one on top of the other and rub my middle finger along the top edge of my index finger to get a yes or no answer to any question. To get a yes answer, my middle finger would slide easily along the index. To get a no answer, my middle finger would stop like it had brakes on and not move if the answer to my personal question was a no answer.

I have found before and since the conference that I am more aware of where I should be in relation to everything else going on around me. I find things I am looking for more easily and quickly by just allowing myself to visualize where the object might be and it is shown to me like I am watching a movie.

So, getting back to paragraph one and the toilet, water closet or bathroom lavatory story, on our first tour to see a famous Gothic Church our guide took us inside.

He was constantly talking about everything except where we might find a bathroom after such a long ride of 45 minutes. Instead of listening to the history of this centuries old church, I was busy looking for a symbol of the ladies'/men's room, or something, and could not find anything.

I was kind of getting panicky because I know I cannot ride to the next stop while not getting to a "pit stop" for myself. I told my husband I could not listen to the guide because finding a bathroom was more important. He tried to help and asked someone. They told him the lavatory was down past the second church altar and to the right. He looked and found nothing. Our friend and trip companion also looked for one, taking his time off the tour guide's informative talk.

I finally found one man who was a vendor selling church souvenirs at the church entrance. I asked him if he knew where a water closet was, he looked down at his table and mumbled, "Past the two altars and turn right." I told him I had already looked and couldn't find it. He repeated himself while being annoyed.

So I told my I AM Presence Self, my dowser body, my body that was magnetic to all I needed that I really need to find a place and I needed, to find it soon because it was urgent indeed. I walked in the direction he told me and saw what I thought was an altar, walked past it and saw another thing like it might be called an altar.

I walked to my right and saw a wall facing me like he told me. I said that guy didn't know what he was talking about. I felt like crying. Then I said to myself, I'll go the end of the wall and see if anything is to the right like he said. I asked myself, "How could anything be back behind this altar." "No way!!!" I walked to the wall, to the right and lo and behold – three or four sinks and to the rear of the sinks, water closets. What?! Lord did I give thanks.

I trusted my promptings and went on faith that I would find what I needed most in life at that time and because of my faith in seeing what was not visible, I learned that my body is a dowsing tool and I can use it as such with my fingers, my subconscious mind and letting myself as a whole be led to be where I was being attracted to be. I allowed my body to dowse exactly what I needed. I wept with thanksgiving. I went to the water closet, came out after washing my hands. Chris saw how happy I was and our companion friends saw me too. They both asked me if I found the lavatory. I said I did. They got so excited because they couldn't find one based on the direction given them by the same vendor.

I joyfully told them I dowsed myself to magnetize one to me and when I did, I found it. They said almost at the same time, "You found one? No way! Show us where" cause now they both had to use it before the group was to leave for the bus. Even when I showed them how to walk to the wall and turn right, it was hard to imagine a water closet would be behind this little narrow opening. I forgot to say the opening was narrow didn't I? Yes – about shoulder's width and then you made a left turn to where the sinks were and to your right were the WATER CLOSETS, narrow as well.

They laughed and laughed and laughed at how I explained the dowsing tool I used which was my body to find the water closet. Hilarious! We all laughed the biggest, fullest, hardiest laugh we had within us AND now people who were pretending to not need the toilets were clamoring to want to know how to get to them.

Another bathroom dowsing method I didn't know existed for me was this. I found this café in the plaza at the end of the street in Sorrento and Chris and I were looking for a place to go again before the bus tour guide had to lead us back onto the bus.

I found a line of women not from our group who had found a set of toilets at the back of the souvenir store of the café. I resigned myself to wait and told myself the guide would just have to wait for me as Chris would not allow them to leave without me.

So I was in line for probably two minutes when a lady from my group ran up to me and whispered "There is a bathroom to the back over there and you don't have to wait!" How was I to know this, were it not for my dowsing mechanism kicking in and magnetizing this information to me? There was no way I could have figured it out. In my mind, I hugged her the biggest hug, and told her I was forever in her debt in my mind! I told her loudly and clearly so she had to have heard me in her heart how grateful and overjoyed I was.

I see all this as my body tuning in to all the answers it needs at any particular time while on our vast tour through France, Italy and Spain. Now we're in Italy and the male guide says "Our trip will take a minimum of one hour and a half. In my mind I go, "What???!!!" I'm thinking to myself, how will I last without a water closet stop? So, halfway through the trip, I whisper to Chris I need to stop somewhere. The guide had just said, if you have any emergencies let me know and I'll see about helping you. So Chris said let's wait and see. I couldn't hold it much longer and he told the guide we had an emergency.

The guide then says, "Can you wait for twenty five minutes, we'll stop at a petrol place and they have restrooms there for you." What?! – I have already waited 30 minutes to tell you, then Chris asked me to see if I would wait for a half hour. and now twenty more minutes. I said to myself, it's a good thing these bus seats are made of flannel because my urine could be absorbed with no tell-tale evidence of having been used. I smiled to myself.

So what I learned on these tours, drink in sips not gulps and certainly not 8 – 16 oz. as I might not find an outlet in time. I learned about being silent for my body to tune into where I needed to be at any one time. One time while in Barcelona, I walked alone to find a place while Chris stood in the bus line waiting for our friends to show up for our local hop on hop off bus tour.

I found cafés that would only let customers use their facilities. I found a wax museum that was still closed to the public and I asked to be shown where the bathroom was. They spoke Spanish not English and I didn't speak Spanish. I finally said in an animated way that I have to *pee pee* and shook my body and that got the message across, so I was shown to a nice water closet. They thought I was interested in paying to see the wax museum and explained it opened at 10 am (which was in about 10 minutes). Funny, funny stuff.

Tune into your body by being quiet and still and your body will show you the ins and outs. The body frequency of the energy flowing through you will attract unto you all you need for your comfort. It will lead you to the right people, the right job/career, the right location/home, the right kind of work, the right non-invasive alternative method of healing for any health condition, etc.

The Universe matches your subconscious mind frequency with the perfect vibrational frequencies you are seeking, believing in and imagining. Conscious mind has no play in this, it is put on the back burner. So allow your body to teach you what it can do.

When you truly visualize, it is God's attribute and power of sight acting on the mind of man. We must determine the desire to be fulfilled.

1. Ask yourself if it is honorable and worthy of your time and effort. Look at your motive – is it honest to yourself and to the world?

Our desire is the expanding activity of God through which manifestation is constantly sustained and is perfection enlarging itself. Make sure you do not have feelings that would make you benefit at the expense of another.

2. State your plan in words as clearly and concisely as possible in the present tense. Write this down or make an audio recording and make this a record of your desire in the outer, visible world.
3. Close your eyes and see within your mind a mental picture of your desire or plan in its finished and perfect condition. This is God's attribute of sight acting in you. God's life and power are acting within your consciousness to propel into your outer world the picture you are seeing and feeling within yourself.

Do not share your desire with others. You become the Law of God. This is God desiring. This is God feeling. This is God knowing. This is God manifesting and God controlling it all. Each spiritual step we take is like going to kindergarten and it prepares us for the next step to graduate school.

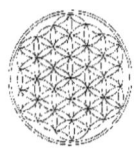

Summary

Your I AM Power has two magical keys called the Two Cups. The two cups are the words I AM. They hold the bounty of your imaginings, your desires. Whatever words you use to fill these two powerful vessels, those are the state of mind that will be displayed, realized, objectified for you in your outer world.

When my goals and desires were not met some 45 years ago, I asked the question of Spirit, why not? I asked why some of my goals were met and why were some of my other goals not met? What was the formula for me to use because evidently I wasn't doing something right? The answer came swiftly.

The answer was basically, I didn't believe it was possible. I put up barriers or doubts, disbelief of why I couldn't reach my goals. Once I heard the secret formula which is what I have shared with you in this book, is that I needed to change my wording. I needed to state my goals in the present tense. I needed to back up my words with feeling, belief, visualization to one of I AM that which I desire to be. I needed to utilize my I AM Power in a positive vein. I needed to fill my two cups with positive words following them or filling them up to the brim with excitement, love, trust and brilliant imagination and visualization. I needed to state the goal as completed, release and let go without anxiety or worry that the goal would not be fulfilled.

I found out through following the Law of Attraction that my dreams could not fail to be fulfilled when I added the "right" wording behind my I AM Power, the right energizing power of my intention and thought.

When I first wanted to begin teaching Hatha Yoga for example, I didn't have any students. So I had to claim, I am so happy that there are people who want to learn from me. I had to claim, I am a great yoga teacher and the universe draws unto me all those who are committed to learning from me.

When my classes started and the numbers in attendance were small, I had to claim, I AM thankful that the class size has increased. And so it was. The class size increased and I had to get a larger building to hold the students. The rent had to be within my budget and my budget kept increasing because I believed it so and claimed, I Am grateful.

Stating things in the present and without needing to know HOW is that possibly going to happen, more things than I could have imagined, happened. They happened quietly for me, "under the covers" so to speak, without my knowing they were to be.

I was invited to give demonstrations, invited to give lectures and introductions on Yoga, invited to start a radio blog show for 5-6 years, invited to produce and direct and host my own TV show for 13 weeks. I was invited to do international radio interviews, magazine interviews and win awards for the work our Doolin Healing Sanctuary was offering for wellness of mind, body and spirit. I eventually wrote a book on Yoga, Meditation and Spirituality for the African American Community: If You Can Breathe, You CAN Do Yoga – The Ultimate Beginner's Book.

If you have a desire within you, it's been placed within your DNA by our Source to become, to BE, so have no doubt that it can be realized. All you have to do is live as if your dream is realized already and do the action steps as they are given you from "under the covers". Trust in your I AM Power to make it so, And It Shall Be So. And So It Is!

Journal

Journal

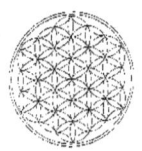

Recommended Bibliography

A Course in Miracles. Published by Foundation for Inner Peace, 19 Windward Rd. Belvedere Tiburon, CA 94920. 1975.

Allen, David. *ASKffirmations: Questions That Create Reality.* Published by Shanon Allen. 2018.

Bartlett, Richard, D.C. and N.D. *Matrix Energetics: The Science and Art of Transformation.* Beyond Words Publishing, (Division of Simon & Schuster, Inc.), 20827 NW Cornell Road, Suite 500, Hillsboro, OR, 97123-9808. 2007.

Benner, Joseph. *The Impersonal Life.* DeVorss & Co., Publishers, P. O. Box 553 Constitution Avenue, Camarillo, CA 93012-8510. 1941.

Benzo, Felicia, *Raising Kings.* Hustle U Inc., Deland, FL. ISBN 978-0-92596-7-5. 2011.

Bucke, Richard Maurice, M. D. *Cosmic Consciousness: A Study in the Evolution of the Human Mind.* E.P. Dutton & Company, Inc. New York, NY. 1969.

Cota-Robles, Patricia Diane. *What On Earth Is Going On?* New Age Study of Humanity's Purpose, Inc. P. O. Box 41883. Tucson, AZ. 1997.

Day, Laura. *The Circle.* Penguin Putnam Inc., 375 Hudson Street, New York, NY. 2001.

Doolin, Daya Devi, Rev. *Super Vita-Minds: How To Stop Saying I Hate You...To Yourself.* Padaran Publications, 1794 N. Acadian Drive, Deltona, FL 32725. 1999.

Doolin, Daya Devi-, Rev. *Dabney's Handbook On A Course In Miracles.* Padaran Publications, 1794 N. Acadian Drive, Deltona, FL 32725. 1989.

Freeman, Tonya K. *Honey Drops: Sweeten the Pot of Life.* Paperback. Amazon. 2017.

Fox, Emmet, Dr. *Power Through Constructive Thinking.* HarperCollins Publishers Inc., 10 East 53rd Street, New York, NY 10022. 1940.

Goddard, Neville. *Your Faith is Your Fortune.* DeVorss & Co., Publishers, P. O. Box 553 Constitution Avenue, Camarillo, CA 93012-8510. 1941.

Hay, Louise. *You Can Heal Your Life.* Hay House, Inc., 501 Santa Monica Blvd. Santa Monica, CA 90406. 1984.

Hicks, Jerry and Esther. *The Law of Attraction: The Basics of the Teachings of Abraham.* Hay House, Inc., Carlsbad, CA. 2006.

King, Godfré Ray. *Unveiled Mysteries.* Saint Germain Press, Inc., 1120 Stonehedge Dr., Schaumburg, Illinois 60194. 1982.

Lin, Chunyi, Gary Rebstock, *Born A Healer.* Spring Forest Qigong Company, Inc. October 1, 2003.

Mulford, Prentice. *Your Forces and How To Use Them.* Publisher, Sun Books / Sun Publishing Company, P.O. Box 5588, Santa Fe, NM 87502-5588, *3rd Printing 1993.*

Murphy, Joseph, Ph.D. *The Power of Your Subconscious Mind.* Prentice Hall, Inc., Englewood Cliffs, N.J. 1963.

Ponder, Catherine. *Prosperity Secrets of the Ages.* Unity Church Worldwide, P.O. Box 1709 Palm Desert, CA 92261-9989. DeVorss & Co., Publishers, P. O. Box 553 Constitution Avenue, Camarillo, CA 93012-8510. 1964.

Wattles, Wallace D. *The Science of Being Great.* Top of the Mountain Publishing, 11701 Belcher Rd., S. Suite 123. Largo, FL 34643. 1983.

Williamson, Marianne. *A Return to Love: Reflections on the Principles of A Course in Miracles.* HarperOne; Reissue edition. March 15, 1996.

Yogananda, Paramahansa. *Metaphysical Meditations.* Self-Realization Fellowship, 3880 San Rafael Avenue, Los Angeles, CA. 90065. 1976.

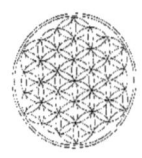

About The Author:

Rev. Daya Devi-Doolin is an Award-Winning and Best-Selling Amazon Author, known as a "Doctor of Thought". She is an American Spiritual Teacher, Lecturer, Entrepreneur, Activist, and Intuitive Counselor. She and her husband Chris founded The Doolin Healing Sanctuary in 1989. They offer safe alternative modalities of healing and certification in Usui Reiki. She is a Certified Usui Reiki Master Teacher and teaches Gentle Hatha Yoga. She has been teaching Yoga since 1970 and is a Registered Yoga Alliance E-RYT 500 Teacher.

Chris and Daya are award – winning recording artists, musicians and songwriters and have authored two books together. She has assisted thousands of clients through workshops, lectures, Radio/TV shows, interviews and personal healings world-wide since 1989. She is the author of eight other motivational/inspirational books. Chris and Daya have two sons, Tyler and Joseph.

www.ingramcontent.com/pod-product-compliance
Lightning Source LLC
Chambersburg PA
CBHW071724040426
42446CB00011B/2203